MW00490065

KEEP
WRITING.

KEEP
FIGHTING.

KEEP USING
YOUR VOICE.

THIS JOURNAL BELONGS TO:

Women's Rights Are Human Rights

★ ★ ★ ★ ★

THEY TRIED TO BURY US. THEY DIDN'T KNOW WE WERE SEEDS.

Mexican proverb

NASTY
WOMEN

TOGETHER WE RISE

Grab 'em
by the
patriarchy

←——————→

Nevertheless, She Persisted

BUILD
BRIDGES
NOT
WALLS

RESIST HATE

★ ★ **★** ★ ★

WOMEN HOLD UP HALF THE SKY.

Mao Tse-tung

Don't Hate, Educate

WE WILL NOT BE SILENCED

I'M WITH HER

—————

LOVE
TRUMPS
HATE

—————

★ ★ ★ ★ ★

IF YOU'RE NOT OUTRAGED,
YOU'RE NOT PAYING ATTENTION.

KEEP YOUR
FILTHY LAWS
OFF MY
SILKY DRAWERS

FIGHT
LIKE
A GIRL

MAKE AMERICA KIND AGAIN

⟨⟵————————⟶⟩

STRONGER TOGETHER

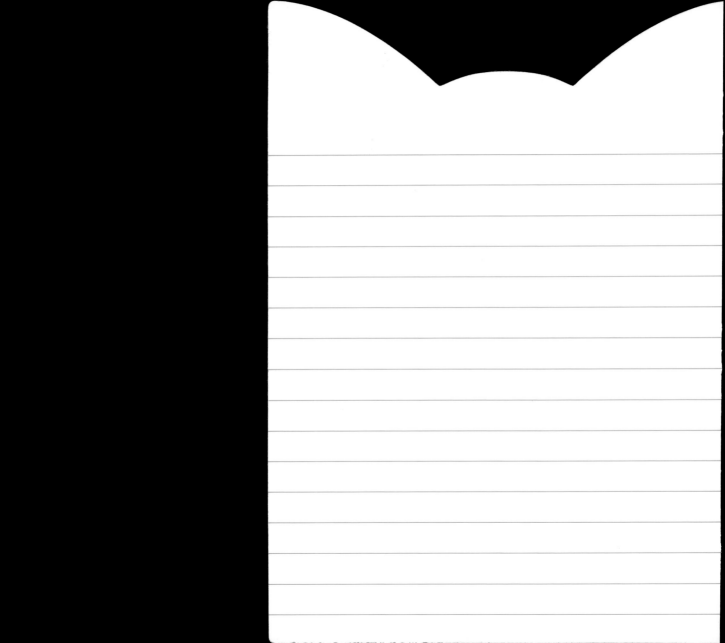

I WILL NOT
APOLOGIZE
FOR WHO
I AM

★ ★ ★ ★ ★

AND THOUGH SHE BE BUT LITTLE, SHE IS FIERCE.

Shakespeare

———

BLACK
LIVES
MATTER

———

The Future Is Still Female

⟪⟶⟫

I didn't come from your rib, you came from my vagina

←——————→

★ ★ ★

SISTERS ARE DOING IT FOR THEMSELVES

RESPECT EXISTENCE OR EXPECT RESISTANCE

⟵⎯⎯⎯⟶

RAISED TO RISE

POWER
TO THE
PUSSY

We Are All Immigrants

Empowered Women

Women

EMPOWER WOMEN

YES WE CAN

We
Should
All Be
Feminists

It's About All of Us

OUR BODIES,
OUR MINDS,
OUR POWER

★ ★ ★ ★ ★

LOVE IS LOVE IS LOVE IS LOVE IS LOVE

VIVA
LA
MUJER

(LONG LIVE WOMEN)

Stay Nasty

STAND OUT, STAY LOUD

LITTLE GIRLS
WITH DREAMS
BECOME
WOMEN
WITH VISION

GET IN FORMATION

Girls just wanna have fun-damental rights

⟵⟶

★ ★ ★ ★ ★

STILL I RISE.

Maya Angelou

I AM WOMAN, HEAR ME ROAR

★ ★ ★ ★ ★

HERE'S TO STRONG WOMEN–MAY WE
KNOW THEM, RAISE THEM, BE THEM!

RESOURCES

VOTING

Check if you're registered to vote
or register to vote: http://vote.org
Find your elected officials:
www.commoncause.org/take-action/
find-elected-officials/

CIVIL RIGHTS

American Civil Liberties Union
(ACLU): https://www.aclu.org
Center for Constitutional Rights:
http://ccrjustice.org
Southern Poverty Law Center (SPLC):
https://www.splcenter.org

CRIMINAL JUSTICE REFORM

Centre for Justice & Reconciliation:
http://restorativejustice.org
The Gathering for Justice:
http://gatheringforjustice.org
Prison Policy Initiative:
http://prisonpolicy.org

EDUCATION

Disability Rights Education & Defense
Fund: http://dredf.org
The Education Trust:
https://edtrust.org
National Education Association:
http://nea.org
Stand for Children: http://stand.org

GENDER VIOLENCE

National Coalition Against Domestic
Violence (NCADV):
http://www.ncadv.org
Rape, Abuse & Incest National Network
(RAINN): https://www.rainn.org

GUN CONTROL

Coalition to Stop Gun Violence (CSGV):
http://csgv.org
Everytown for Gun Safety:
http://everytown.org

HEALTH & REPRODUCTIVE RIGHTS

Center for Reproductive Rights:
https://www.reproductiverights.org
NARAL Pro-Choice America:
http://www.prochoiceamerica.org
Planned Parenthood:
https://www.plannedparenthood.org

IMMIGRATION

National Immigrant Law Center (NILC):
https://www.nilc.org
National Immigration Forum:
http://immigrationforum.org
National Immigration Project of the
National Lawyers Guild:
http://nationalimmigrationproject.org
UN Refugee Agency (UNHCR):
http://www.unhcr.org/en-us

LGBTQ

Human Rights Campaign (HRC):
http://www.hrc.org
National LGBTQ Task Force:
http://thetaskforce.org
Parents, Family & Friends of Lesbians &
Gays (PFLAG): https://www.pflag.org
Sylvia Rivera Law Project:
https://srlp.org
Transgender Law Center:
https://transgenderlawcenter.org
TransWomen of Color Collective
(TWOCC): http://twocc.us
Trans Youth Equality Foundation (TYEF):
http://www.transyouthequality.org
The Trevor Project:
http://www.thetrevorproject.org

POLITICAL ENGAGEMENT

Center for Community Change:
http://communitychange.org
Common Cause:
http://www.commoncause.org
Indivisible:
http://indivisibleguide.com
Our Revolution:
http://ourrevolution.com

RACIAL & RELIGIOUS JUSTICE

Americans for Indian Opportunity:
http://aio.org

Americans United for Separation of
Church and State: http://au.org
Anti-Defamation League (ADL):
http://adl.org
Asian Americans Advancing Justice (AAJC):
http://advancingjustice-aajc.org
Black Lives Matter:
http://blacklivesmatter.com
Council on American-Islamic Relations
(CAIR): https://www.cair.com
League of United Latin American
Citizens (LULAC): http://lulac.org
Mexican American Legal Defense
and Educational Fund (MALDEF):
http://www.maldef.org
The Movement for Black Lives:
https://policy.m4bl.org
National Association for the
Advancement of Colored People
(NAACP) Legal Defense and
Educational Fund: http://naacpldf.org
National Congress of American Indians
(NCAI): http://ncai.org
National Council on U.S.-Arab Relations:
http://ncusar.org
Race Forward:
https://www.raceforward.org
Urban Justice Center's International
Refugee Assistance Program (IRAP):
http://irap.urbanjustice.org

SCIENCE & ENVIRONMENT

Citizens' Climate Lobby:
   http://citizensclimatelobby.org
EarthJustice:
   http://earthjustice.org
GreenPeace:
   http://greenpeace.org
350.org:
   http://350.org
Union of Concerned Scientists:
   http://www.ucsusa.org
World Wildlife Fund (WWF):
   http://www.wwf.org

WOMEN IN POLITICS

Emily's List:
   http://www.emilyslist.org
She Should Run:
   http://sheshouldrun.com

WOMEN'S RIGHTS

National Organization for Women (NOW):
   http://now.org
National Women's Law Center (NWLC):
   http://nwlc.org
Women's March on Washington:
   https://www.womensmarch.com

POTTER

crownpublishing.com
clarksonpotter.com

Copyright © 2017 by Clarkson Potter

All rights reserved.
Published in the United States by Clarkson Potter/Publishers,
an imprint of the Crown Publishing Group, a division of
Penguin Random House LLC, New York.

CLARKSON POTTER is a trademark and POTTER with colophon
is a registered trademark of Penguin Random House LLC.

ISBN 978-1-5247-6307-7

Printed in China

Conceived by ROBIE LLC
Cover and interior design by Jessie Kaye

10 9 8 7 6 5 4 3 2

First Edition